# From Solo to Supported

## A Writer's Guide to Finding Community

Jessie L. Kwak

Microcosm Publishing
Portland, OR | Cleveland, OH

# FROM SOLO TO SUPPORTED
## *A Writer's Guide to Finding Community*

Part of the Good Life Series

First Edition, 3,000 copies
First published October 2025
ISBN 9781648412547
This is Microcosm #787
Edited by Lex Orgera
Cover illustration by Lindsey Cleworth
Book design by Sarah Koch and Joe Biel

For a catalog, write or visit:
Microcosm Publishing
2752 N Williams Ave.
Portland, OR 97227

All the news from the misprints in print at www.Microcosm.Pub/Newsletter

Get more copies of this book at www.Microcosm.Pub/FromSolotoSupported

EU Safety Information: https://microcosmpublishing.com/gpsr

To join the ranks of high-class stores that feature Microcosm titles, talk to your rep: In the U.S. COMO (Atlantic), ABRAHAM (Midwest), BOB BARNETT (Texas, Oklahoma, Arkansas, Louisiana), IMPRINT (Pacific), TURNAROUND (UK), UTP/MANDA (Canada), NEWSOUTH (Australia/New Zealand), Observatoire (Africa, Europe), IPR (Middle East), APD (Asia), HarperCollins (India), and FAIRE in the gift trade.

Did you know that you can buy our books directly from us at sliding scale rates? Support a small, independent publisher and pay less than Amazon's price at www.Microcosm.Pub.

Global labor conditions are bad, and our roots in industrial Cleveland in the '70s and '80s made us appreciate the need to treat workers right. Therefore, our books are MADE IN THE USA.



Library of Congress Control Number: 2025024909

**Microcosm Publishing** is Portland's most diversified publishing house and distributor with a focus on the colorful, authentic, and empowering. Our books and zines have put your power in your hands since 1996, equipping readers to make positive changes in their lives and in the world around them. Microcosm emphasizes skill-building, showing hidden histories, and fostering creativity through challenging conventional publishing wisdom with books and bookettes about DIY skills, food, bicycling, gender, self-care, and social justice. What was once a distro and record label started by Joe Biel in a drafty bedroom was determined to be *Publisher's Weekly's* fastest growing publisher of 2022 and has become among the oldest independent publishing houses in Portland, OR and Cleveland, OH. We are a politically moderate, centrist publisher in a world that has inched to the right for the past 80 years.

LETTERPAPER
WATERS

# TABLE OF CONTENTS

# From SOLO to SUPPORTED

## A WRITER'S GUIDE TO FINDING COMMUNITY

JESSIE L. KWAK

MICROCOSM PUBLISHING
PORTLAND, OR CLEVELAND, OH

21
22
23

# IT TAKES A COMMUNITY

One of my favorite parts of any book is the acknowledgments.

I mean, I love getting lost in the story and absorbed in the prose. I love bonding with characters and learning new facts and exploring complex ideas. But I really, really love that moment at the end when the author pulls back the curtain and gives the world a peek at how much community goes into writing a book.

The average acknowledgments page includes people like editors, critique partners, teachers, and mentors who helped get the dream across the finish line. It also tends to include folks like neighbors and family members and friends and babysitters—all the people around a writer who supported and enabled the dream. And, of course, there are almost always shout-outs to the nebulous cloud of writer friends and groups who inspired and encouraged the writer, and kept the dream alive in the most frustrating hours.

If you've only seen depictions of a writer in popular culture, you could be forgiven for thinking we're all reclusive loners, hermitted away in our cabins in the woods while we work on our magnum opus. But the truth is that almost all successful writers are surrounded by a web (a network! a constellation!) of people who are critical to their journey.

Yes, the main requirement of writing is to sit alone with one's thoughts. But that doesn't mean writing has to be a solitary pursuit. Instead, it can happen with the support and encouragement of a vibrant, uplifting community.

In fact, I would argue that community isn't just nice for writers to have. It's actually a huge part of what will make you successful (whatever your version of success looks like). Your writing skill, your perseverance, your mindset—all of that matters. But your community is the electric current that will keep you going for the long term.

They say success is all about who you know—and they're right.

Your community will help you professionally. They'll tell you about opportunities, invite you to submit to anthologies and promo opportunities, and introduce you to people who will open doors.

Your community will hone your craft. They'll critique your work, challenge you to write better, hold you accountable to your goals, and inspire you to push yourself in new directions.

Your community will support you personally. They'll hear you when you need to vent. They'll celebrate your wins with you. They'll get it when you have some weird writer-specific complaint, like how your characters aren't behaving and have totally derailed your plot.

Success is all about who you know. But I don't want you to feel like that's a barrier. I want you to see it as an opportunity.

Because you, too, can build a writing community that supports you in the tough times and celebrates with you in the good times. You can make connections with people who will become your collaborators and introduce you to opportunities. You can construct a thriving, healthy network that will make your writing more fun and fruitful, whether you're pursuing a professional career or simply enjoy writing as a hobby.

I know this idea might seem intimidating, especially if you're shy and introverted—and let's face it, a lot of writers are. But don't worry. You don't need to become a master schmoozer or have been born with a zillion Charisma points to build your writing network.

How do I know? Because when I was in my early twenties, I didn't know anyone who wrote speculative fiction. I was an incredibly shy kid. I was terrified of introducing myself to strangers and would get tongue-tied any time someone asked me to talk about my writing.

Here's the secret: I still am. But I've learned to manage that fear. And one person at a time, one encounter at a time, one brave step at a time, I've surrounded myself with a writing community that Jessie from twenty years ago couldn't have even imagined.

If I could teach myself how to enjoy networking, believe me, you definitely can.

We'll talk about how in a minute. But first, let's take a step back from that mercenary word "network" for a second and talk about what it really means.

## *Forming a Stellar Writing Constellation*

What we're really talking about here is your community, the interconnected circles of people you know and who know you. Some of them might be your closest confidants—the people you trade drafts with and share your deepest joys, fears, and frustrations with. Others might be acquaintances, people you know on a friendly level and enjoy chatting with but don't go out of your way to grab coffee with. Some might be professional connections, the editors, podcast hosts, agents, and other industry pros you might have met once or twice and (hopefully) made a good impression on.

All of these people are stars in your writing constellation. Some closer in, some farther out—all your connections.

I emphasized "your" in the last sentence because I want to make an important point before we get too much farther into this book.

You can absolutely find a pre-existing community and plug yourself into it, but please don't stop there. There's a whole wide world of potential writer friends out there waiting to join your constellation, and you should assemble them in a way that supports you—instead of dimming or reshaping your own light to meet someone else's expectations.

On occasion, I hear a new writer say something like, "I tried to meet other writers, but it didn't work. I joined a writing group, but they were..." Unwelcoming and cliquish. Dismissive of genres that aren't their own. Pedantic and inflexible. Brutal and unhelpful in their critiques.

Whatever the reason, a new writer had a bad experience with a writing group and figured that they were better off on their own than hanging out with other writers.

Maybe that's happened to you, too. Personally, I've had more run-ins than I can remember with groups (and individuals) who rubbed me the wrong way or with whom I wasn't a good fit—and that's okay. The good news is that the writing community isn't homogenous. Which means that instead of having to file off the things that make you you in order to fit with a specific group, you get to pick through the options to build your own unique ecosystem that helps you thrive.

In other words, if you limit your community horizons to a single critique group or writer's association, you'll be stuck conforming to their social mores and cultural norms, even if it's not the best fit for you or your writing. If, instead, you cultivate a robust network of groups, associations, and individual writer friends that come from different places, you'll have a stronger sense of yourself, and you won't give away too much influence to one specific group.

In other words, don't join a cult!

(Kidding. Kind of.)

But even if you've found a really good group right off the bat, it's not likely to have everything you need.

A critique group and a business mastermind group don't perform the same function. Friends you make at a literary conference versus a sci-fi fan convention will support you and your writing in different ways. You'll meet a different slice of the writing world at a weekly write-in than you will at a weekly reading series.

Why not explore them all?

When you focus on forming a writing constellation all of your own instead of plugging into an existing community, you'll have a lot more agency and confidence as you navigate the vast world of writer groups out there.

When I say "form your own constellation," I'm not necessarily suggesting that you need to go out and start your own critique group or social meetup or workshop—though that's a fantastic idea if you're up for it. I'm talking about building your own ecosystem of friends and sub-groups within the larger selection of writing groups available to you. That gives you the flexibility to assemble a crew that supports you and offers what you need, and allows you to shine and give back in a way that supports them, too.

You're the star in the center, surrounded by a unique grouping of other stars. Some of those points of light will be individual stars you meet within the community. Some points of light (just as in the constellations we see from Earth) will actually be star clusters like critique groups and workshop cohorts, or even galaxies like professional organizations and conferences.

You and another writer may run in similar circles, but your constellation will necessarily be unique from theirs because you're standing at the center of it. You're the one who chooses how to move among these starry skies in the way that best supports you.

## *Anybody Can Do This!*

What if you've never gone to a single writing event or spoken with another writer? No worries! Anyone can build a writing community.

This book is meant to be part how-to guide and part inspiration to get you out and connecting with other writers. It's packed with direct, actionable advice that you can use immediately. Along the way, I'll share bits of my own story (and how I've managed to get past my own crippling shyness), but mostly I'll stay focused on helping you assemble a toolkit that will boost your confidence as you navigate networking for writers.

We'll start off by exploring the different places where potential new writer friends tend to congregate and talk about how to join those spaces. Then, we'll get into the nuts and bolts of social encounters with other writers—including preparing for a networking event (physically and mentally), rocking the event itself, and following up afterwards.

We'll also talk about the sometimes tricky gray area where personal and professional relationships can overlap with writer friends, and how to navigate those gracefully. And, finally, we'll discuss how to make sure your constellation is filled with healthy, uplifting stars rather than energy-draining black holes.

A whole world awaits! I know you'll be able to find a writing community that will support you, lift you up, guide you, present you with opportunities, and be an amazing source of energy, inspiration, and friendship along your writing journey.

It's all about who you know. So let's start getting to know some folks.

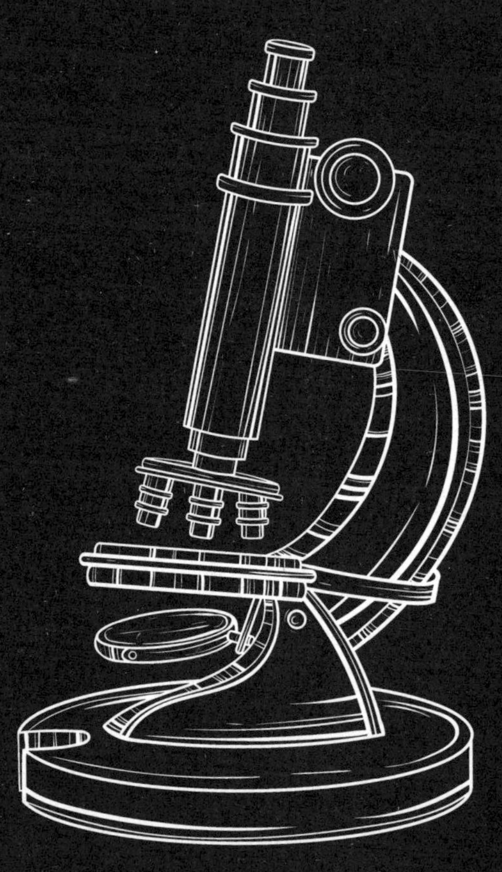

# CHAPTER 1: WHERE ARE ALL THE WRITERS?

Meeting other writers isn't like joining a bowling team or a board game club—hobbies which require interaction with other humans in order to even exist. Writing tends to be pretty solitary, and the natural habitat of writers is in our own heads, in front of our laptops, ensconced in our lairs like dragons.

So how do you even find other writers to connect with? Fortunately, as a species, writers can sometimes also be found congregating in well-known watering holes and traveling well-worn game trails. You just have to know where to look and be willing to jump into the fray yourself.

The good news is that even if you live in a small town, the internet has made it possible to connect with people who not only write but who write the same sorts of things you do. No matter your niche or sub-genre, you can find other writers who share your interests, and you can start making those connections.

And with every connection you make—every star you add to your constellation of writer friends—you'll learn about new write-ins and meetups and conferences and Discord groups and professional forums where you can sink even deeper into the community.

In this chapter, I'll give a brief overview of the places you might meet other writers.

Remember, as you explore different groups, some may resonate and some may not. If a particular conference, workshop, or social media hashtag doesn't click with you, let it go and keep exploring.

You may eventually find a group or two you want to officially join, or you may not. But you'll definitely collect friends for your constellation along the way, and, like we just talked about, that's the more important part.

## *Creative Writing Classes and Workshops*

Many people I know—myself included—made their first writer friends in a creative writing class or workshop. This might be in high school or college, though there are plenty of opportunities to take creative writing classes or workshops outside of formal schooling.

Many community colleges offer non-credit elective classes that are open to anyone. When I first moved to Portland, I took a short story writing class from a local author who has since become a friend. I also ended up forming a short-lived critique group with a handful of people I met in that cohort of students.

Different writing organizations in your area may also offer classes. Depending on how big a city you live in, those organizations might draw in some pretty exciting authors for you to learn from, too!

Of course, you can also take writing classes online, though if your goal is to meet your classmates, make sure you sign up for a class that has a social component to it—that could be regular video calls, critique exchanges, small group work, an active forum, or anything else that gives you an opportunity to get to know other writers in the class.

Another option is to attend a multi-day workshop. These can be even more effective for forming connections with your fellow students, since you'll often have after-hours activities and social time to get to know each other. You may find these workshops in your area, or you might consider traveling to attend one in a fun location.

Workshops range in time commitment from one day to one weekend (like the three-day critique workshop held by Cascade Writers), one week (like Viable Paradise), or multiple weeks (like Taos Toolbox and Clarion). Note that some of the more prestigious workshops tend to have robust application processes and require you to submit writing samples.

Another, less structured option, would be to look for writing retreats or residencies, where a group of writers take a mini-vacation to spend some quality time with their writing. While there's normally a lot of solo writing time involved—that's the point of these retreats—many will have a social element with shared meals and other activities.

## *Critique Groups*

Critique groups are a wonderful place to meet other writers while improving your craft. They range from vast online networks like Critique Circle (which has thousands of members) to small, hand-picked groups. Some are ongoing, others meet at a regular cadence, and yet others are one-off events (like a critique group session at a conference). Some require every author to submit work each meeting, others leave it more random.

No matter the format, critique groups are a fantastic way to share your work in its early stages, get feedback, and develop relationships with other writers.

One of the first critique groups I joined was Critters.org, which is an online critique group specifically for writers of science fiction, fantasy, and horror. You submit your story in manuscript format to a queue, and when its time comes, Critters members can choose to read it and give feedback.

I quickly learned that I got just as much value (maybe more) from critiquing other writers' work as I did from reading their critiques of my own manuscript. It's a great way to learn what works, what doesn't work, and why—because you have to articulate that to the author.

Around that same time, I also formed my own small group with three other Seattle-area authors I'd met at a conference. We called ourselves the Shining Creamsicles (for reasons that are lost to time). Brian, Jesse, Natasha, and I met monthly to have dinner and talk writing for several years until life changes drifted us one-by-one out of Seattle.

These early critique groups were instrumental in building confidence in my writing and honing my craft, as well as helping me meet people I still consider my friends to this day.

A little googling should help you find groups of writers who critique work in your genre, either online or local to you. You could also try searching Meetup.com or Facebook for local in-person critique groups. Finally, writing conferences (which we'll talk about in a minute) often also have a critique group component attached.

## *Mastermind Groups*

Critique groups exist to help you hone your craft. Mastermind groups exist to help you hone the business side of writing.

Just like you'd share early drafts with a critique group, you can share business ideas with a mastermind group. You can talk about your goals, share your successes and setbacks, and know that there's a group of people ready to celebrate with you or offer support when you need it.

(Having a writer group-chat that you can gripe in on occasion is way better than airing grievances on social media and potentially burning bridges, by the way!)

If this sounds interesting to you, you can form your own mastermind group by recruiting a few real-life or online friends. You might meet formally and have a set agenda of sharing challenges and successes, or you might just spin up a group chat or private forum to share ideas. You could also join a more formal mastermind group—both self-organized or part of paid membership programs—that you discover online or through your network.

I found mastermind groups to be immensely helpful when I was first starting out. (I still do, in fact. While I rarely use critique groups these days, I'm a member of several strong mastermind groups.)

The first mastermind group I joined was the Freelance Writer's Den, a paid forum for freelance writers. There, I learned the ropes of the business, asked newbie questions, and met people I still consider friends to this day. Three of us who met on that forum spun out into a weekly accountability group where we posted our goals for our business, shared our wins, and asked for support through our challenges. Forming that group with Ayelet and Stephanie was one of the best things to happen to my early freelance career.

You can have mastermind groups that aren't just writers, by the way. My longest running mastermind is with my friends Andrea and Nalisha, who are a knitting pattern designer and artist respectively. We've been checking in weekly for over a decade on our goals and achievements.

The most important thing is to find people who share your values, have a similar level of drive, and who you trust enough to share intimate details of your business. (Some masterminds require you to sign non-disclosure agreements because of this.)

## *Write-In Groups*

Still other groups get together to—gasp—write! This could be a few hours a week at a coffee shop or library, or even for days on end at a writing retreat, as mentioned above. They don't exchange work to be read (though you can generally arrange that with individuals if you like) and they don't teach craft or business (though there's normally a lot of shop talk when writing isn't happening.)

The main point of the meeting is simply to sit down and write together.

If you haven't done it before, I highly recommend writing alongside other people! The accountability of watching everyone else's fingers flying on their respective keyboards is powerful. Even if you're feeling stuck, it's hard to tab over to social media and start scrolling when everyone around you is productively working those word mines.

Most write-ins have a specific format designed to help you be productive while also leaving time to socialize. They generally will have a timed writing session (25-50 minutes), followed by a break for chatting, followed by another writing session.

How can you find these writerly gatherings? Start by checking different organizations in your area to see if they host a write-in. For example, the public library might have a write-in, or a group might meet at a local coffee shop or bar. If you have a local writing association, they might host public write-ins. Meetup.com can also be a good place to find write-ins in your area.

Online write-ins can also be quite helpful, and often follow a format that includes time to socialize and get to know your fellow writers via a video call. Poking around on social media or searching a website like Reddit for write-ins in your specific genre is a good way to connect with these.

Can't find anyone hosting a write-in? Start one yourself! Contact your local library or pick a coffee shop or bar with plenty of seating, then post about it in local forums and ask if you can post a flier about it at the business itself.

If nothing else, just start showing up every week with your laptop and a sign that invites others to sit at your table and type away.

I met my oldest Portland writer friends because I was writing in public at a local coffee shop soon after I'd moved into town. Erik, the organizer of a local write-in at the Vancouver library, happened to be sitting next to me. He noticed that I was using the word processing software Scrivener, and since it's a pretty niche tool used mostly by novel writers, he politely introduced himself and asked if I was working on a novel.

When I said yes, he invited me to the monthly write-in he hosted. I made a point to attend and quickly found myself plugged into a lovely group of people who have since formed the core of my writer friend group in the Portland area.

## *Conferences and Conventions*

Writing conferences and conventions are also fantastic places to start building your writing community. Walking into a big room full of strangers can feel overwhelming, but don't worry, we'll talk about strategies for rocking that in a later chapter.

When you're looking for a conference, keep in mind that there are different types. Some focus on specific genres—literary fiction, nonfiction, sci-fi and fantasy, thrillers and mysteries, horror, romance, etc. If you're writing a memoir, you might have a hard time connecting with people at a mystery writers conference, and vice versa.

These conferences also vary in how they approach publishing. Some cater more to indie and self-published authors, while others focus on finding agents and selling books to publishers. Any writer can gain valuable information from either, but it helps to know where your "tribe" is and to be aware of a conference's publishing approach and genre focus going in.

Additionally, some conferences focus more on craft, while others focus on the business side of writing. Some are geared toward beginners, while others are aimed at more established authors. And if you're a copywriter or blogger, you'll want to find a conference that's specific to business writing rather than fiction.

If you have the means and opportunity, it's worth traveling to attend a particular conference that sounds like it would be a good fit. When I heard about the Smarter Artist Summit years ago, I was in a place where I was desperate to meet other indie authors. I took the leap, and traveling to Austin for the conference turned out to be one of the best things I did for my career. I met some of my closest writer friends there, and the conference's focus on building an uplifting community eventually inspired me to start my own similar event in Portland.

Of course, you'll also find plenty of online conferences these days—and some do a better job than others at fostering community. If that's what you're looking for, I recommend reading reviews or contacting the organizers to see what kind of networking opportunities they offer.

For example, when the Willamette Writers Conference went virtual in 2020 due to COVID-19, I was glad they were still offering presentations but disappointed about missing my favorite part: the opportunity to network. They announced a virtual happy hour event as part of the conference, and I logged on reluctantly, expecting it to be dull.

Not at all. Kate Ristau, Willamette Writers' executive director, hosted a brilliant format on Zoom. For the first hour, we were thrown into random breakout rooms every ten minutes, where we got to introduce ourselves and chat with two or three other people—like speed dating for writers. For the second hour, we got to choose our own breakout rooms, so we could track down the people we'd connected with most and continue the conversation.

By the end of the virtual happy hour, I'd met dozens of people, some of whom I remained in touch with and became friends with. It was shockingly fun!

## *Social Groups (Online and In Person)*

Finally, there are groups of writers who meet just to chat and socialize, rather than for any specific agenda. Local writing organizations might host socials or happy hours, or you might end up spinning off a board game night or social club from a more writer-focused critique group or workshop you attend.

Online, social media can act like one massive writers' happy hour. This makes it a great place to connect with other writers—but also a great way to waste a ton of time! So please be self-aware about why you're logging onto your social media of choice. Are you deliberately cultivating community? Or are you just scrolling to unwind? Whatever you're there for, make sure you get the writing done before you open the app or tab.

One way to connect with other writers on social media is through hashtags and writing challenges. Whatever ones are popular at the time I write this sentence will surely be defunct by the time this book comes out, so I encourage you to search out hashtags and challenges on your social media of choice.

Another way is to join a group or forum organized around a topic or sub-genre that you write in. You can find public groups on places like Facebook and Reddit, and when you start to make virtual writer friends you can ask them for recommendations and get invitations to private writing social groups on places like Discord and Slack.

Substack is another lively place to connect with other writers. What was once just a newsletter service is becoming a real community, where writers and readers can share and discuss each other's work. Many Substackers also host meetups and clubs for their communities.

Some writing associations also host forums for members, which can be a lovely way to connect with people writing in your genre or niche.

## *Readings and Literary Events*

Another great place to meet people is at local events for other writers. If you see that one of your favorite authors is coming to town for a reading, chances are other writers who also admire that author will be there. You can strike up a conversation with people sitting around you before or after the reading, or while standing in the signing line.

Your local bookstore, coffee shop, or bar might hold regular literary events such as readings or open mics. These can sometimes be better places to meet your fellow writers than a big-name author event, because they tend to draw a small community of the same people each time.

This is one area where I found it much, much harder to actually network with people online. Online readings can be great, and you can certainly chat in the comments, but it's not the same as having a chance to sit around with a cup of coffee or a beer after an open mic. Or even chat with someone randomly in line at the cash register before the event begins.

That said, going to online readings and engaging with people in the chat can sometimes lead to connection. If you genuinely feel like you've developed a rapport with someone, it's worth sending them a direct message explaining that you are looking to connect with other writers and asking if they would like to meet for virtual coffee.

## *Take Action*

Make a list of the various places you might meet other writers in your area (or online). Begin by jotting down the places you already know of (like a local reading series or writing conference), then add to that list by searching for things like "write-in [my town]" or "creative writing class [my town]" or "online critique group [my genre]."

If you already have a few writer friends or belong to a writing forum online, you can also reach out to ask what suggestions they might have for events you could attend or groups you could join.

Keep in mind that each group (and each writer friend) will tick different boxes for you. You might have a group of friends (or a formal group) who exchange critiques, and another, separate, group with whom you can talk about the craft and business of writing. You might share stories about your process, bounce ideas off each other, and support one another—but never actually read each other's work.

No one group—or one person—needs to tick every box. It's all part of the constellation, after all!

Now that you know where to find new writer friends, let's talk about one of the biggest hurdles for a lot of folks: putting yourself out there.

# CHAPTER 2: PREPARING FOR A NETWORKING EVENT

I hemmed and hawed about using the phrase "networking event" to describe write-ins, classes, meetups, and the other shenanigans us writers get up to. The word's got a bad corporate rap, and I was worried it would conjure up images of people wearing blazers and heels and "Hi my name is" stickers whipping out stacks of glossy business cards and pitching each other on their startups.

I didn't want anyone to throw this book out and head for the hills.

So many of us writers are introverts who enjoy spending our free time lost in our own worlds, telling stories to ourselves within the comfort of our own heads. The classic "networking event" is the polar opposite of that happy place.

But writer networking events aren't like that, and that's a very good thing. You don't make new friends by working a room and tossing business cards around like confetti. You make friends by having great conversations about writing with other interesting people—which, for most writers, ends up being pretty fun.

Think of it like a party! There's just one big difference: a networking event is a specific type of party where the explicit goal is to make new friends rather than only hanging out with the ones you already have.

The act of networking is really just building your community in a focused, intentional way. When you attend a writer-focused event with the goal of finding new stars to bring into your constellation of writer friends, you're networking.

And, yes. Walking into a crowded room and introducing yourself to a stranger requires a very different skill set from sitting alone at your desk having conversations with imaginary people and trying to figure out the exact right word to describe the taste of Red Vines on the first day of summer break. But don't worry—it's a learned skill. And if I can learn how to do it through trial, error, and perseverance, you can learn how to do it, too.

So let's call a networking event what it is, and reclaim the idea of being a good networker!

Being a good networker starts well before you walk into a write-in, social meetup, or conference. I'm going to talk through how to prepare yourself, but first I want to offer two mindset shifts that might come in handy.

Small shifts in your mindset can have a huge impact on how comfortable you are at a networking event. These shifts probably won't happen quickly, but they will absolutely happen if you keep working at it. I excused myself from multiple networking events in my twenties in order to have a quick meltdown and panic attack in the bathroom before returning to continue socializing. I left multiple events early because I couldn't talk myself down from the anxiety and just needed to get out of there.

But I kept going back. I kept practicing. Eventually the panic attacks went away and the social anxiety ebbed. And, most shockingly, I realized I'd learned to enjoy diving into a crowd of strangers and working the room.

It's possible to shift your mindset. And though it's well beyond the scope of this book to help you overcome deep-seated social anxiety and related problems, I want to give you a few tips to get you moving in the right direction. If you feel like you need more professional advice in order to work through your shyness and self-confidence, there are tons of excellent resources out there—books, courses, coaches, and therapists.

(*Unf#ck Your Brain: Getting over Anxiety, Depression, Anger, Freak-Outs, and Triggers with Science* by Dr. Faith G. Harper is a good place to start.)

You've got this!

## Mindset Shift 1: Let Go of Ego

Do you worry you're too shy, awkward, or weird to meet new people? Let me tell you a secret. You may often have felt isolated from people who didn't understand you or your writing—but we writers are all a bunch of weirdos. You're in the perfect community!

Yes, there are bad apples who might make you feel unwelcome, but for the most part the writers I know are extremely understanding and friendly. We're patient with shyness because we're mostly all introverts. We're cool with quirks because we're all quirky. We're forgiving of social awkwardness because we're all socially awkward.

Come hang out!

If you find yourself worrying about what other people think about you—whether you said the right thing, did the right thing, wore the right thing, or made a fool of yourself—that's natural. But it's also wasted energy.

It's just your ego talking.

We normally think of someone with too much ego as being puffed up and self-aggrandizing, but too much ego can trip us up in the other direction. It can make us feel self-conscious and worried that everyone in the room is secretly judging us. In both cases, it's the ego trying to protect its fragile self by building strong walls and shark-filled moats between us and other people.

I guarantee people aren't spending nearly as much time as you imagine analyzing your performance at a networking event. We're all too busy picking apart our own missteps and stewing over our own awkwardness. In short, most people are too busy dealing with their own ego battles to remember that embarrassing thing you said last week, even as your own ego is driving you bonkers over it.

If you really did make a mistake—you said something you later understood was hurtful, you made another guest feel uncomfortable, you spilled a drink on someone—then you need to address it with the person who was affected. Clear the air, make amends, and move forward like adults.

But if you notice your ego chattering about things that aren't a big deal and holding you back from comfortably interacting with people, take a moment to feel what you're feeling, acknowledge that it's a valid response, thank your ego for trying to help keep you safe, and then release it so you can focus on what really matters.

Meditating has become my go-to for dealing with my own social anxiety and self-recriminating monkey mind. I don't have a super consistent practice, and it never feels like I'm "getting better at meditating" during the ten-ish minutes I sit a few times a week. But, over time, it's become clear that the repeated practice of stepping outside my own monkey mind has helped me gain a more realistic view of what's actually going on and turn down the volume on my fragile ego.

## Mindset Shift 2: Embrace Imposter Syndrome

Wait. Who even are you to walk into this room with all these other writers?

These real writers?

If you experience imposter syndrome, this thought has almost certainly bounced through your head. It might have kept you from going to writer events in the past or from enjoying yourself fully while you were there.

Imposter syndrome is the self-doubt someone feels about their professional ability—even when faced with evidence that they're absolutely qualified. It's what keeps us from applying for jobs, submitting to writing contests, applying for raises, accepting invitations from agents to send them manuscripts, or saying "thank you" when someone compliments our stories.

It's the feeling you might get when you look around the room at a conference or other networking event and think, "Any second, the organizer is going to walk over and say, 'Sweetie, I'm sorry, but this is an event for writers. You're going to have to leave now.'"

As far as I can tell, the only way to deal with imposter syndrome is to ignore it and keep doing what you need to anyway. That's because if imposter syndrome is one of your recurring stories, it's never going to completely go away.

Once you become comfortable introducing yourself as a writer and shut down that particular imposter voice, another one might pop up when you find a critique group and feel like your feedback isn't good enough. Once you get comfortable offering critiques, that imposter voice will diminish—but it will return in full force when you start querying editors and agents or applying to speak at conferences.

Let me tell you from experience—there's no cure for the imposter voice, just like there's no cure for any self-critical voice in your head. You'll keep doing bigger and more important things to prove it wrong, and that voice will simply find a new angle of attack.

You just have to do the work to ignore it.

Learn your personal self-sabotaging stories and their triggers. Talk about them with friends and therapists. Keep a journal of your wins, chronicling your journey as you methodically check off things your imposter voice says you'll never be able to do. And just keep trucking.

One valuable thing I've learned from imposter syndrome is that it can drive me to be more professional. For example, when I didn't feel "good enough" to speak at a local conference, I asked myself, "What does someone who is 'good enough' look like? How do they act? How do they present themselves?"

Asking those questions gave me a reasonable checklist to compare myself to. A "good enough" speaker has a great topic idea. They present themselves professionally online. They often have written books, blogs, and essays about the topic. They show their experience by giving smaller presentations and volunteering to be on programming at other conferences.

I realized I'd checked most of the boxes already—I'd spoken in front of smaller groups of people, I'd written books on the topic, I presented myself professionally. The main thing I didn't know how to do was craft a great topic idea and pitch it, but that was a skill I figured I could learn.

Once I'd worked through my checklist and shored up the places where I felt weak, I knew I was ready to submit proposals to speak, and whenever the imposter voice tried to speak up, I could just point at the work I'd done.

This doesn't mean you need to do extra work every time imposter syndrome rears its head.

You probably already check all the boxes—especially if you're from a disadvantaged community where imposter syndrome is especially insidious. Historically, the people traditionally held up as "professionals" have been cis (probably male), straight, white, and neurotypical. If you didn't grow up seeing people who looked like you being successful writers, that voice of doubt can scream all the louder.

In the end, it's about learning to take steps despite the fear. It's about understanding what this particular defense mechanism is protecting you from or trying to teach you, and acting anyway.

That voice may never go away, but you can learn to give it a little patronizing pat on the head as you head out the door to greatness.

Oh—and before we move on? Let me just tell you this:

If you are writing, you're a real writer.

If you write but are currently in a slump, you're a real writer.

If you're just learning how to write, you're a real writer.

Now let's get ready to go!

## *Dress for Success*

I was a theater kid in high school. I was never a great actor (I preferred the technical side of things), but I did take a few turns on the stage. And let me tell you, something magical happens when you put on a costume.

During normal rehearsals, you're up on stage pretending to be Elizabeth Proctor from *The Crucible*, trying to put yourself in the mind of a beleaguered Puritan woman whose husband's mistress is accusing you of witchcraft—all while dressed like a nineties grunge kid in frayed secondhand corduroys and a flannel.

Then comes dress rehearsal.

Suddenly, you're in a plain gown and apron, your hair pulled back tightly under a bonnet, wearing makeup that adds two decades to your face. You not only look more world-weary and brave—you feel it. Instead of a nineties teenager freaked out about SAT scores and college applications, you're suddenly transported back to the life-and-death tragedy of the Salem witch trials.

It's a magical moment to put on a costume and slip into a character—whether on stage or in our everyday life.

Putting on a costume is a skill we use every day, even if we don't call it that. Have you ever noticed how your entire attitude and body language sometimes shifts when you put on a certain piece of clothing? We put on our favorite ratty band T-shirt to get energized for chores. We put on fancy shoes for a nice dinner, or toss a professional shirt over our tank top for a Zoom meeting with a client. We have special items in our closet that make us feel smarter and tougher, masc or femme, playful or serious.

So why not have a networking costume that helps you get into character?

This costume should:

- Be comfortable
- Make you feel most like yourself
- Boost your confidence
- Be a good fit for the crowd you're networking with

Checking these boxes will look different for different people—and it will probably look different for you as your style and confidence evolve.

It will also probably look different depending on the event you're attending. If you're attending a networking event for business writers, you'll probably step it up more than if you're going to the Monday night write-in at your local brew pub. If you're at a writer's conference in Portland, Oregon, jeans and a fleece pullover count as formalwear—not so much in New York City.

But for the most part, writing network events are casual. You can't go wrong with jeans and a T-shirt, especially one that supports your favorite fandom or has a writerly pun on it.

Ten years ago, my networking "costume" looked a little more formal than it does today. Back then, I was trying to project a more sophisticated, mature persona. I cultivated a lightly gothy, business-casual vibe—pencil skirts and heels, with my own funky (often hand-sewn) twist.

Those outfits gave me the confidence to approach people, even though I still felt like an impostor sneaking into these events. They were a kind of armor, helping me play the part.

These days, I'm not trying to trick myself into feeling like I belong, so my costume has gotten more casual. My go-to uniform at the moment is a pair of black skinny jeans, silver sparkle Doc Martens, a comfortable top, and a statement necklace—usually with a black jacket over it all.

Putting a little thought into your uniform can boost your confidence, give you an easy conversation starter, and help people remember you at future events. But most importantly, this part should be fun. It doesn't have to be fancy or complicated. You probably already have a uniform—it's just a matter of refining it for these events in a way that boosts your energy and confidence.

## *Wear a Statement Item*

Having a statement item in your arsenal (like the sparkle Docs and necklace I mentioned above) can be invaluable. First, it can make you feel fun and fancy, like a secret talisman that gives you social networking energy. Second, and more practically, it offers other people something interesting to comment on.

A statement item is a built-in conversation starter. I can't count how many conversations I've had with strangers over the years that started with, "Oh wow, I love your boots!" or "That's a great necklace!" or "I love your glittery eye patch!"

It becomes a natural icebreaker and provides an immediate point of connection. Think of it as an offering to someone who might want to start a conversation with you. Walking up and saying, “Hi, what do you write?” is awkward for everyone. But if you see someone wearing a T-shirt with a quote by your favorite author on it, it provides you with an excellent conversational opening gambit.

Finally, having a statement item in your networking uniform can also contribute to your author brand. By “brand,” I just mean it helps people remember you as that person who always wears book-themed dresses, or the person with the blue hair, or the person with the rainbow eyeglass frames.

A statement item doesn’t have to be fancy or flashy. One of my students at Cascade Writers last summer showed up every day wearing a T-shirt with a different clever writing pun. He always got a laugh and started a conversation. A friend of mine wears a very cool bracelet made out of a bass guitar string, which gets comments (and ties into his books). Another friend has a galaxy-print button-up he wears to more "formal" events.

## *Do Your Research*

Before the event, spend some time figuring out what you want to get out of it and who you might want to meet. (Whether a specific person or a category of person, like "other picture book authors.") Are you just hoping to meet people in your area? Are you hoping to connect with writers in your genre to form a critique group? If you're going to a writing conference, is there a specific speaker whose work you admire and you hope to get an autograph from?

Some events publish lists of attendees, which gives you a chance to do a little light googling to see if anyone there might be a good connection—maybe they write in the same genre or do similar copywriting work. This can help you go in with a plan for who you want to connect with.

You don't have to reveal that you've done your homework if it feels awkward. In fact, it might be better not to, unless it comes up naturally in conversation.

Years ago, I attended a week-long business masterclass with about fifty people. A fellow attendee greeted me by asking, "What kind of hops did you use to dry-hop that beer?" When I gave him a confused look, he clarified that he was talking about a photo on my website's About page, from when I waitressed at the Elysian Brewing Company and the brewers let me help pour some hops.

It turned out he wrote for beer magazines, and we became fast friends. But I was initially startled that someone knew so much about me before I even got their name.

So, do your research, but maybe don't lead with obscure facts that show you've been googling them.

## *Be Connectable*

Look. I know I said writer networking wasn't about schmoozing and passing out business cards like a club promoter passes out free drink coupons. But it's really not a bad idea to print up some business cards and keep them on you at all times. They're really one of the easiest ways to tell people how to connect with you once you've hit it off.

A good business card could be as simple as your name, title (Writer of Fantastical Adventures with a Twist of Romance!), website, socials, and preferred way to be contacted. You could glam the whole thing up with some stock imagery and a tagline, if you want.

Keep your networking cards fairly simple and timeless. A box of one hundred will probably last you years, so pick something you won't mind handing to strangers and industry professionals for a while to come.

While you might also have a pack of business cards with your book covers on it, I highly recommend also just having some networking business cards. (After all, you're at these events to meet writer friends, not to sell your books to new readers.)

There are some interesting business card alternatives out there, like bracelets people can tap with their smartphones to add your contact info to their phone. It's also perfectly great to exchange phone numbers if appropriate, or follow each other on whatever social media platform you both use in common.

Another great option that works in a pinch is to save a QR code on your phone that links to your website, so a new acquaintance can scan that.

Whatever you decide, don't assume you'll just remember people's names and websites-slash-contact info. If someone doesn't have a business card, jot down their contact info in a physical notebook or a notes app so you can move on to the next conversation with a clear mind, rather than worrying that you'll forget how to get ahold of the person you were talking to before.

## *Take Action*

Set a timer for twenty-five minutes and journal. How are you feeling as you think about attending your next writer networking event? What stories are popping up? What can you do to make yourself feel more prepared?

Maybe that's as simple as checking to make sure your hair isn't sticking up at a weird angle, then doing a quick power pose in the mirror. Maybe you need to schedule regular time for journaling or meditating to get that self-critical voice in your head to calm down a bit. Maybe you need to book time with a therapist or a friend to talk through some more deeply entrenched stories that are keeping you from putting yourself out there.

Whatever you do, please don't view the suggestions in this chapter as ways to avoid walking through the door! Don't let "order business cards" or "buy a new T-shirt with puns on it" be the excuse to keep you from going out and building your community.

Because you're already enough. Good enough, smart enough, brave enough, and prepared enough. Now let's go rock us some networking events.

# CHAPTER 3: ROCKING THE EVENT

You've picked out a writing meet-up. You've signed up for a conference. You've enrolled in a workshop.

You've chosen your networking event, and you've prepared for it as much as possible. (Or, frankly, as much or little as you felt like!)

It's time to walk in and make some writer friends.

In this chapter, we'll cover the art of wading into the fray and having a fun conversation with a fellow writer or five. As I mentioned in the last chapter, a networking event is really just a party where the goal is to talk to strangers and hopefully move a few of them into the "friend" or "acquaintance" region of your writing community constellation.

It should be fun!

But you're also there for a purpose—which is why I want to make you aware of one of the main things you can do to sabotage yourself.

## The Friend Trap

The Friend Trap is extremely seductive, because it always feels more comfortable to attend an event with a friend. Knowing a friend will be there can give you the courage and accountability to show up in the first place. And, if all else fails and there's no one worth talking to, you'll know at least one person at the event to chat with.

But I've watched too many writers show up to an event with a friend (or romantic partner) and never talk to anyone else. If your goal is to have a fun thing to do with your friend, that's fantastic. But if your goal is to make new writer friends, you need to be deliberate about talking to people you don't know. Sometimes, having a friend there makes this goal much harder.

As well as logistically keeping you from meeting strangers, attending with a friend can subtly shift the way you act. (This is especially true if you're attending with a non-writer romantic partner.) When you're in a group with someone who knows you well, you tend to act slightly differently than when you're on your own—especially when you're early in your networking journey and still learning how to push out of your comfort zone. Getting out of that comfort zone can be easier to do in a room full of strangers than it is when someone who knows you is watching.

Let me give you an example.

My husband is far more outgoing than I am. He enjoys being the center of attention, whereas I do not. When we're at an event together, I don't have to step up and be the social one—I can just relax and let him work the crowd. But when I'm on my own, I have to leave my comfort zone and learn how to be the extroverted one. It forces me to put myself out there in ways I normally don't.

The first time we both understood this dynamic was a few years into our marriage at a meet-and-greet for our new neighborhood. My husband was arriving later, so I showed up by myself and timidly wandered into the crowd of strangers. I figured I wouldn't talk to anyone until he arrived, but by the end of the hour, I'd become fast friends with a little crew of neighbors who were about our age.

We were all laughing and joking together when my husband showed up. My back was to the door, so I didn't see him. He rolled in and leaned against a pillar next to me—quite close—and announced his presence with: "Well, hello, gorgeous."

One of our new neighbors immediately took a step forward with his chest puffed out. "And who are you?" he demanded.

My husband lifted his hands and stepped back, startled, and I reassured our neighbor (who is actually an incredibly gentle—and quite protective—puppy dog of a human) that this was the husband I'd been talking about.

Later, my husband remarked on how quickly I'd made friends who liked me enough to fight for me. I was shocked at the same thing, because I always thought I was the quiet, introverted one. But it turned out that when I wasn't relying on the crutch of an extroverted friend or partner, I could unlock an inner extrovert of my own.

If you do go to a networking event with a friend, make sure they know your goal is to meet new people. Create a plan that allows you to spend some time together, but also split up to network. You could even make it a game—see how many people each of you talks to by the time you meet back up for lunch. This is a great way to double the reach of your constellation-forming efforts.

## Joining the Conversation

As I've said a dozen times already, a lot of writers are introverts. This means we often worry about bothering people by approaching them to strike up a conversation. But when you're at a writer networking event, the good news is that most writers there don't know how to talk to each other, either—so if you can learn to be the one who breaks the ice, you'll be doing everyone around you a favor.

Just think about how grateful you feel when you're sitting alone, unsure how to join a conversation, when someone comes up to invite you to talk.

You don't have to wait for that person. You can be that person.

While this would be awkward in a coffee shop, the beauty of a networking event is that everyone's there to meet new people. It's not weird to walk up to a group of folks who are chatting at a conference, or sit down next to a classmate in a workshop and say, "Hi, I'm [name], mind if I join you?"

Most people will be cool with that. If they're cliquish or standoffish—maybe they're caught in the Friend Trap—that's their loss. Brush it off and go find someone who's interested in expanding their circle of friends.

So, what do you say once you've found yourself a conversation partner?

Sparking up a conversation and keeping it rolling is a skill—a skill you can most definitely learn. Having a few conversation starters in your back pocket is a great way to feel more confident.

## Talk About Writing

At a writing event, you've already got a built-in point of connection: writing. You can ask about what kind of writing they do or what they're working on lately.

- What are you currently working on?
- How long have you been writing?
- What's the best piece of writing advice you've heard?
- What genre do you write? What draws you to it?

## Talk About the Event

Another strong point of connection is the event you're both at. You can ask what brought them to the event or what they're hoping to learn. If there are speakers or readings happening, you can ask what they thought about them.

- What brought you here today?
- What are you hoping to get out of this event?
- Have you attended this event before?
- What did you think of [speaker or reading]?

## Talk About Books

If you're in a room full of writers, you can bet you're in a room full of readers. This can be another solid place to start a conversation, especially if you share a love of the same genre.

- Have you read anything good lately?
- What authors inspire your writing?
- What was your favorite book as a kid?

- What's on your to-read list that you're most excited about?

## Talk About Life

Another good opener is to ask a question that's a little unusual but not too personal like, "What do you do for fun?" or "What have you been excited about lately?" At this point, though, it's best to keep things fairly surface-level.

Ask questions that allow your conversation partner to control the depth with which they respond—you'll sometimes hear people at business networking events ask things like, "What are you passionate about?" and while there's no shade if you've ever asked that, it can feel like a lot of pressure. It puts the person on the spot and can make them overthink their answer.

- What do you like to do when you're not writing?
- What do you do for work?
- What do you do for fun?

- What have you been up to this [summer/fall/season]?
- What have you been excited about lately?

### Talk About Their Statement Item

In the last chapter, I suggested wearing something that sparks conversation and gives people an opening with you. If you see someone with a clear statement item—rad shoes, a book-themed skirt, earrings made to look like their favorite classic novel—complimenting it can be a perfectly fine place to start.

I'll just throw out this caveat: if you worry that complimenting the item would be construed as a come-on (like commenting on a cute but tight-fitting dress), steer clear. Shoes, jewelry, and funny T-shirts are safe bets.

### Talk About the Weather

Sure, it's basic, but it's something you both immediately have in common. You both arrived at the event in the same weather conditions. And if the weather is particularly weird, you might even have a funny anecdote to share. It's a fast, easy way to find a point of connection, which you can then move on from.

## *Going Deeper*

Small talk often gets a bad rap for being insubstantial, but it serves an important purpose. It helps establish a baseline connection you can build on. Becoming friends with someone is all about finding those connections and creating stronger links over time.

But, obviously, if you can't move the conversation beyond the weather, you probably won't become close friends—and that's okay. You don't need to have a great conversation with everyone.

When you do want to go deeper, here are some tactics for digging in.

### Ask Open-Ended Questions

Encourage people to go beyond simple yes and no responses by asking questions in a way that requires a longer response. For example, if someone mentions a movie they just saw, instead of asking, "Did you like it?" ask, "What did you enjoy about it?" or "Were there any techniques you saw that you'd want to use in your own writing?"

Listen, and follow up on responses: We've all been in conversations where it's clear the other person is just waiting for us to stop talking so they can talk about themselves instead. Don't be that person. Don't spend the time rehearsing what you'll say next. Make your conversational partner feel heard by actually listening to what they're saying and asking follow-up questions.

## Find Out What Lights Someone Up

A fun question to invite connection is some variation on, "What gets you excited about [whatever they just mentioned]?" or "How did you get into [whatever hobby or genre they brought up]." It's lovely to see someone's eyes light up when you give them a chance to share what they're really into.

## Explore the Whys and Hows

Questions about why or how are great for digging deeper. For example, "Why did you first become interested in writing [genre]?" or "How does your day job subject matter play into your writing?"

## Find Common Ground

Throughout the conversation, keep looking for places where you can build rapport and share your own experience. Try to do this in a way that keeps inviting them to share, rather than using it as an opportunity to take over the conversation. For example, "You're working on a memoir? So am I! How have you approached structuring your story?"

## Avoid Fraught Topics

It's a good idea to steer clear of politics, religion, and other hot-button issues. You can't assume everyone shares your worldview, and the last thing you want to do is create a space where another attendee feels attacked or excluded. Highly political jokes or comments are best avoided, even if you think you're in a group where people probably mostly agree with you.

Of course, if you're someone for whom a shared political or religious ideology is a key prerequisite for a friendship, that's a completely different story. But if your goal is to broaden your network, it's important to assume that other people don't share your biases. After all, as writers, we're here to explore different perspectives, not push an agenda. Broadening your own horizons means learning to have productive conversations with all kinds of people.

## *Talking About Yourself*

At some point in any conversation with other writers, you're going to get asked about your writing.

Personally, I hate this part. I interview people regularly for my day job, and I sometimes find myself approaching social conversations in the same way. I'm great at asking people questions that invite them to talk about themselves for hours. But the moment someone asks me what I write, my brain seizes up—even after all these years.

You're going to be asked what you write over and over again, so I recommend you not follow my example of simply deflecting to a different topic. Instead, figure out a way to respond gracefully. If you're someone who hates talking about your writing, practice opening up and sharing. If you're someone who loves talking about your writing, practice not monopolizing the conversation.

When someone asks some variation of "So, what do you write?" you should have a few canned responses in your back pocket.

## Elevator Pitch

Have a short elevator pitch ready—under a minute—and practice saying it until it feels natural. This should include your genre and a bit about what you're working on currently. For example, "I write action-adventure sci-fi stories. Right now I'm working on a book that combines my love of Firefly with my love of cons and heist stories, about a plucky band of criminals that fly around the system doing crime for good."

## Longer (but Still Quick) Summary

Once you give the fast-and-dirty elevator pitch, your new writer friend might say, "That sounds cool. How did you enjoy the speaker?" In which case, you're free to move on to other topics. But they also might ask for more details about what you're working on. If so, you'll need a version of your pitch that expands on the idea.

However!

Your longer version should still be pretty short and snappy, hitting your main characters, the central conflict, and explaining a bit about where the story is going. Think of it like the back cover copy for your book.

For example, "My story follows Lasadi, the captain of the Nanshe, who's an exiled freedom fighter on the run after her planet's failed war of independence from the Alliance. She's a loner, but she's forced to bring on a crew for this heist—and one of the people she hires is this guy named Raj. She figures out pretty quickly that he fought for the Alliance during that war, but she thinks he defected, so she's willing to work with him—but she plans to keep an eye on him. Fortunately, he's pretty easy on the eyes. *Wink!* Of course, he's got a big secret—but so does everyone on this new crew. Because this is the first book of an ongoing series, it's all about getting the crew together, and how they learn to trust each other despite their pasts and the secrets they're keeping."

Save the detailed world-building or blow-by-blow of the plot for a later conversation. (Or, for if they seem genuinely interested and keep asking you questions.) Please don't just dive into a thirty-minute discussion of your magic system or historical research project—even if someone expressed interest at first. It's very easy to go from "Wow, that sounds interesting!" to "Will this person stop talking?" in a matter of minutes.

Practice the art of knowing when to stop and ask about the other person's work. If you're only talking about yourself, it's not a conversation.

## *Ending the Conversation*

The nice thing about networking events is that it's easy to end a conversation without it being awkward. You can simply say, "Well, it was great to meet you! I'm going to keep mingling." If you want to keep in touch, exchange contact info, and then move on.

You don't need a pretext like, "I'm going to refill my drink" or "I'm going to check out the snacks," though those work just as well.

Sometimes, you might get stuck with someone who's monopolizing your time, whether they're telling you their entire trilogy plot or going on a political rant.

It can be hard to extricate yourself from this, especially if you've been socialized to be polite and not hurt anyone's feelings. But remember, if someone's monopolizing your attention and hasn't asked you a single question, they're the one being rude. You're not being rude by shutting the conversation down.

You're no one's therapist here. You don't have to listen to them. Feel free to interrupt to say you need to keep mingling, and walk away.

## Take Action

How ready do you feel to dive into conversation? If you feel like some prep work would help, spend some time brainstorming conversation starters, and jot them on a card to keep in your pocket during the event. You probably won't need them, but it's a trick that might make you feel more confident.

Write out a couple versions of your elevator pitch. Practice a short-and-sweet version that you can fire off when someone asks what you're working on, as well as a more in-depth answer that doesn't go too far off the rails. You can practice in front of a mirror, or with a friend (writer or not).

As a final bit of encouragement, let me share my friend Daniel's philosophy on networking: The people you're looking to meet are also looking for you. Us writers are a group of weirdos (in the best way possible!), so no matter how much of an odd duck you feel like you are, there are people in this community who share your specific passions and quirks and joys.

And they've been waiting their whole lives to meet you.

# CHAPTER 4: FOLLOWING UP

You made it through the networking event! You met some cool folks. You swapped some business cards or social media handles. You've got some prospects—either in the friend department, or in the professional relationship department.

What do you do now? Send 'em a little note to follow up.

A lot of what you're doing at networking events is tossing out seeds that may (or may not) grow into a fruit-bearing friendship. You sparked up a delightful conversation and enjoyed talking with each other. You exchanged contact information and the mutual intention of keeping in touch.

Now it's time to lightly water those seeds and see which ones start sprouting.

To some people (raises hand), this step can feel just as scary as walking into a room full of strangers in the first place. I'm guessing I'm not alone, given how few people actually follow up with me after we meet, even if I've explicitly asked them to.

This is imposter syndrome rearing its ugly head again.

So-and-so said she would love to get coffee, but she was probably just being nice. And that guy who said I should email him to learn how to submit to the anthology he's editing was only being polite.

"An agent asked me to send them a query even though their website says they're closed to submissions," a friend recently told me. "So I don't know if I should. They probably said that to be nice."

Reader, they did not.

If someone tells you to email them, do it. I frequently tell people, "Shoot me an email and let's chat more about [insert topic, probably self-publishing or the business of writing]." But the percentage of people who take me up on it is in the single digits.

Believe me. If I've told you to email me about a certain topic, it's because I am honestly interested in talking more about that topic with you. I'm not being nice—I have learned hard lessons about being nice to people I don't actually want to talk to.

So, follow up! Be the person who takes initiative and moves the conversation forward, and you'll definitely stand out—in a very good way.

## *When to Follow Up*

I recommend following up within the first day or two after an event. If it takes you almost a week, you're still doing great—but I wouldn't let it go longer than that.

Of course, if you do let it go longer than that, don't use your tardiness as an excuse not to follow up at all. Better late than never. We all have hectic lives and understand that things slip through the cracks. Just send something like, "Sorry for the delay in following up, but life got away from me since we met at X conference! If the offer's still open, I'd love to join your coffee shop write-in. When are you meeting next?"

The whole process of following up shouldn't take you too long, even if you've met a good handful of people at an event. Set a timer for thirty minutes, and work your way down the list of people you had a connection with. Send them an email. Follow them on the social medias, if that's your jam. Forward them the name of that book you mentioned. Then move on to the next person on your list.

### Pro-Tip

It's a great idea to take notes about things you need to follow up with while you're at a networking event. That could be sharing a book recommendation or forwarding the link to a resource you talked about, or even sending the first few pages of your manuscript to a potential critique partner.

I also often jot down quick notes about who I met and things that I want to remember about them, so that when I get home, and it's all a blur, I have something to help me remember that the horror writer I met is John and the cybersecurity marketing writer is Lourdes. I like to carry one of those little spiral bound notebooks that fit in your back pocket, along with a cheap clicky pen.

It's totally appropriate to make follow-up notes in front of someone: "I'll send you that podcast when I get home! Let me just write that down so I don't forget." It's a bit weirder to make notes about people in front of them. "So your dog's name is Ender and you have three siblings in North Dakota, interesting. Hold on, just adding that to my notebook. Don't worry, I'm not a serial killer. I promise."

If you're one of those awesome organized people, go through your event notes as part of your follow-up step, and make sure they're entered into whatever system you use to track things. I recommend reading Tiago Forte's excellent book *Building a Second Brain: A Proven Method to Organize Your Digital Life and Unlock Your Creative Potential* to learn more about staying on top of your notes.

If you're me, and your note-keeping system is a completely unfathomable disaster even after reading *Building a Second Brain*, feel free to do a quick round of emails, and then throw your notes in a drawer where you'll never look at them again. It's all good.

## What Should You Say?

Remember, you don't have to take too much time with these follow-up notes. Quickly reiterate where you met (especially if it's been more than a few days), mention what connected you, and express your desire to stay in contact. This is also the time to send them anything you said you would. (Hopefully you jotted that down in your notes!)

Be sure to personalize each note so that it comes across as authentic, instead of as a generic networking blast.

> *"It was nice to meet you at the write-in at Rose City Book Pub last week. It's great to get to know other fantasy authors in the area, and I appreciated our conversation about worldbuilding. Hope to see you at the next write-in!"*

If you had a good rapport with someone, you can suggest something more proactive than "Hope to see you soon!" Suggest a video call, in-person coffee date, or extend them an invitation to another event you'll be attending.

> *"It was nice to meet you at the write-in at Rose City Book Pub last week—I always love meeting other fantasy authors. I'd love to grab coffee sometime and continue our conversation about the challenges of worldbuilding if you're interested!"*

When suggesting a next step, be clear that you'd like to hang out more—but don't be pushy. Be respectful of the person's time and obligations and give them an out to reschedule if they don't currently have the bandwidth to pursue new friendships.

This is also a great time to share something that adds additional value, or encourages the conversation to continue—like an article or resource related to the conversation you had. Note that there is a fine line between adding value by linking to an article, and assigning someone homework. Just like when you're suggesting a coffee date or virtual meet-up, be clear that any "additional reading" you're sending is optional.

## *What to Do If They Don't Respond*

Not everyone will respond to your follow-up emails. Maybe they're slammed with work. Maybe they're in the middle of a family or health crisis. Maybe they're just really disorganized and terrible keeping on top of their inbox.

And maybe they really were just being nice to you at the event and are brushing you off now.

Whatever the reason, there's no way for you to know—so don't take radio silence personally. Everybody is dealing with circumstances that are outside your control and that are probably far bigger than you.

If keeping in touch with them isn't the biggest deal to you, feel free to let it go. But if you really felt like you had rapport (or they requested your follow up email) and you haven't heard back after a week or so, it's absolutely okay to send a second note to check in.

If you're polite and give them the benefit of the doubt, most people will appreciate a nudge. I certainly do!

But if someone doesn't respond to your nudge, don't keep poking at the relationship. It's still probably not personal—and it's definitely not worth worrying about. And you also run the risk of coming off like a stalker by continuing to email into the void.

## *Ongoing Maintenance*

Some friendships go straight to one hundred out of the gate. Others take time and repeated effort to get the wheels spinning. Even if your initial invitation to grow the friendship doesn't pan out due to scheduling conflicts, take time every few months to ping interesting folks that you've built a bit of rapport with. Check in on how they're doing, share things that reminded you of your conversation, or chat about industry news.

> *"Hey there! I just read this article, which reminded me of our conversation about lichens of the Pacific Northwest. I hope you're doing well! Let me know if you're interested in grabbing coffee and writing together sometime in the next month or so."*

To keep this kind of follow-up respectful, be aware of how (and how often) they respond. If they didn't respond to your email last month, or the one three months before that, they're probably not going to respond to the next one. It's time to let them go. If they legit just sound busy right now and encourage you to reach out again in a few months, take them at their word.

You can't force a healthy and supportive writing constellation, you can only encourage its formation. Some people will immediately soar into your inner circle. Others will linger around the edges as friendly acquaintances. Still others will keep on their own path—and that's just fine. Save your energy for the folks who reciprocate.

## *Take Action*

Decide how you'll take notes on things you need to follow up on at your next networking event. An app on your phone? A physical notebook where you jot down potential writer friends? In Sharpie on the back of your hand? (Been there, done that.)

Then schedule thirty to sixty minutes on your calendar after the event for follow up. Set a timer, pour yourself a cup of coffee or tea, and work your way through the list. You can also schedule monthly check-in times and go back through your notebook to see if there's anyone you've built rapport with that you'd like to check in on.

See? That wasn't so bad after all.

Now that you're starting to gather writer friends, let's dig deeper into how to navigate the unique challenges of being friends with a bunch of writers.

# CHAPTER 5: NAVIGATING PERSONAL RELATIONSHIPS

Being friends with writers comes with unique considerations. A healthy writing constellation can be an incredible source of joy, support, and inspiration. But it also requires you to manage personal friendships that blur the boundary into professional relationships in ways that other friendships normally don't.

Think of it like a Venn diagram. There's the professional circle of people you'll know in the writing community with whom you have a purely business relationship. There's the personal circle of people who are purely your writer friends. And then there will be folks who fall in the middle of the diagram. People you consider friends but also have professional business relationships with.

People may flow in and out of this center slice of the diagram as circumstances change. For example, you might suddenly have a professional relationship with someone you previously only considered a friend:

- Your editor friend might acquire (or reject) your story for their anthology or magazine.
- You might decide to work with a writer friend to co-host a reading or co-write a story.
- You might join a group promotion—like a boxed-set promo or fundraising anthology project—where you have to coordinate marketing with other writer friends.

On the flip side, you might start to develop a friendship with someone (an editor, an agent, a publisher) you previously only had a professional working relationship with.

Even if you're not specifically working with another writer friend, tensions can arise in the friendship because you're both navigating the same arena:

- You might sell a story to a magazine your friend has been rejected from (or vice versa).
- You might get a rejection from an agent the same day a friend announces a three-book deal.
- You might dearly love hanging out with a writer friend and agree to beta read their book, and it turns out you don't like their writing.

Building a strong and healthy writer constellation around yourself requires good awareness of how these professional and personal boundaries interact so you can protect yourself, protect your friendships, and thrive together.

Let's take a closer look at the different places you need to keep an eye on.

## *Balancing Friendship and Criticism*

It's not easy to listen to someone tear apart your story—even if they're doing it in a loving, professional way. That's why strong boundaries and self-awareness are especially important when mixing friendship and critique.

There are a number of ways critique can show up in a writer community. You may be a member of a formal critique group, like we discussed in Chapter 1. You might reach out to a few people whose opinions you value as a one-time thing to ask them to beta read a piece for you (either from the perspective of a fellow writer or as a subject matter expert—like someone who knows about nuclear physics or has lived experience with a group that's outside your own). Or, you might develop an ongoing one-on-one critique partnership with another writer.

However you find yourself giving or receiving feedback from a friend, it's important to keep it professional.

When asking for critique, set expectations about what you're looking for. Do you want to know if specific aspects of a piece are working? Do you want to hear about typos, or is it too early in your process to bother? Do you want technical feedback and fact checking? Do you just want to hear how the story landed for the reader overall?

When you're giving a critique, the number one rule is to be kind. Your role is to help another writer improve their craft, not tear down their self-confidence. Yes, helping someone improve their craft means being honest. But if you aren't able to offer feedback without being brutally honest and mean, you probably aren't at a stage where you should join a critique group.

It's important to understand that just because you're friends with another writer doesn't mean you're the right audience for each other's work. You might agree to critique a friend's story or novel, and find that a) it's fine but it just doesn't land with you or b) it's a mess and you're not sure how to politely say that.

If it's the former, it's totally okay to say that you're not the right reader for the work and offer what feedback you can anyway. If it's the latter, try to be gentle in pointing out overall strengths and weaknesses, and maybe aim your friend at some resources where they can learn more about character motivation, plotting, pacing, etc.

Try to critique a short story (or sample chapter) before agreeing to take on a whole novel for someone if you haven't read their work before. But if you have agreed to read a novel and you just can't get through it, it's also fine to give them a partial critique. I once had a critique partner tell me he stopped reading my novel after he realized he was just noting the same few issues over and over again. This saved him time, but it also saved me time because I didn't have to wait any longer for his feedback. I wasn't offended in the slightest—he was nice about it, and his feedback was spot on.

(If you're thinking, "But if my critique partner doesn't read the whole novel, they won't understand the earlier parts!" keep in mind that an agent or reader will be much less gracious than a critique partner when it comes to making it to the end of your book. Take the feedback about where they stopped reading and use that to craft a book that hooks readers the entire time.)

As a general rule, when you're critiquing a piece you should focus more on your reactions and less on offering prescriptive solutions. What worked for you? What did you love? What knocked you out of the story? What didn't ring true to life or match up with expectations that were set earlier in the story? Where did things seem inconsistent or confusing? Where did you want more detail? Less detail?

When you're in the critic's chair, it's also important to set aside your own assumptions about what you think the author is doing and examine your own biases as you offer feedback. Are the "rules" you're applying to your critique actually set in stone? Or are they actually stylistic guidelines specific to your subset of genre, or lived experience?

Sci-fi writer Mary Robinette Kowal teaches people to use the ABCD method of critiquing:

- What was Awesome?
- Where were you Bored?
- Where were you Confused?
- When did you experience Disbelief?

If you're interested in learning more about being a good critique partner or beta reader, I highly encourage you to read some of her essays on the topic.

## *Working with Other Writers*

There are all sorts of fun ways to collaborate with writer friends. You can co-edit anthologies! Set up a reading series! Write a book together! Organize a writing retreat!

But with every opportunity for a fun collaboration comes a potential way to derail a perfectly good friendship.

Working with friends can be rewarding, but it requires solid communication skills, clear ground rules, and lots of trust and respect from the get-go.

No matter how close you are personally, treat a collaboration like you would a business proposition. Be clear on your expectations: for the project, for the amount of time both of you will spend on it, for financial outcomes, for responsibilities. How will you both remain accountable without one of you having to take on the role of taskmaster and creating resentment in the other? How will you handle creative differences or disagreements? Who will be responsible for what, and how will you make sure those tasks get accomplished? If finances are involved, how will that be handled?

I recommend starting with a small project to see how you work together before diving all in. Do you want to start a publishing company with your bestie? Awesome! But maybe try producing a one-off anthology project first. Do you think it'd be fun to write a novel with someone in your critique group?

It probably would be! But maybe try writing a short story together before diving in.

It's also important to draw some boundaries between your business relationship and your friendship. Set up times to work together on your project, but don't forget to set up times to just hang out, too. Yes, personal chat and business chat will probably leak from one container to the other, but if you need to have a tense conversation about a missed deadline, schedule time to clear the air before you crack open your third beer on movie night.

Oh! And definitely draw up a contract around responsibilities, finances, and IP ownership—no matter how small the project or how close your friendship is. Your future self will thank you, even if everything goes swimmingly.

## *Being Friends with Industry Pros*

You might find yourself becoming friends with people like editors, agents, publishers, conference organizers, and others who play a professional role in the writing industry. This can be fun! But it's also extremely important to draw clear lines between their role as your friend, and their work role.

Please don't pursue a friendship with an agent or an editor simply because of their position. One editor friend told me, exhausted, that they never know if a writer they've hit it off with will be a real friend, or if they're just being friendly because they want to submit work. They'd just had what they believed to be a true friendship blow up in their face because their "friend" got mad at them for not accepting a story for their (quite competitive) magazine.

If you do become friends with an industry pro, don't assume they'll give you preferential treatment, and certainly don't expect it or demand it. Be careful not to make requests that might cause them to compromise their professional values, and definitely don't treat them like they're a stepping stone in your career.

In the end, friendship and professionalism will bring you way more success and happiness than stepping on people to get to the top.

## *Dealing with Jealousy*

One thing that doesn't get acknowledged enough in writer friendships is how jealousy can rear its ugly head.

You might end up losing out to a friend for a limited slot in an anthology or a writing workshop. You might be struggling in your own journey to find an agent or finish a novel while a friend is celebrating a three-book deal or a successful book launch. You might be feeling great about your modest book launch, only to have a friend announce that they sold movie rights.

It can be really tough.

It's totally natural to be jealous when you see someone having the success you want, even if they're a friend of yours. It's okay to take a moment to feel bad even as you are happy for them.

But it's not okay to linger on the jealousy and let it sour your friendship.

You have to manage your own feelings here, and do the work to be in a healthy place in regards to your own writing journey and business.

One critical thing to keep in mind is that nobody's journey as a writer takes the same path. There's no one way to be a successful writer, which means that the only thing you can do, really, is to keep your eyes on your own paper instead of comparing your success to other people's—friends or no.

## Protecting Your Creative Voice

As you get critiques on your work, it can be easy to hear writing advice from multiple people and let it overwhelm you or flatten your own voice. Everyone will have their own opinion, which means that for every person you know, you'll hear that many ways you "should" be writing. It's important to know when to listen and when to stick to what feels right for you.

It's also important to know when not to share your creative work. Certain pieces or ideas might be too fresh, and sharing too early might workshop out the parts that make these pieces uniquely yours before you've even had a chance to develop them. Other pieces might be too personal, and sharing them with the wrong people might do irreparable damage to you and to the work.

There's no solid guideline for when a work is ready to share. Some people are ready to workshop their ideas from conception. I tend to need a solid amount of incubation time with a new project before I feel comfortable sharing more than a few details—let alone a draft. It's a matter of personal preference and instinct, which you'll develop the more you write and the more you share your work with others.

As you gather feedback, be careful of trying to incorporate everything you hear. If you let ten people read your story, you'll get ten different opinions on what you can do to improve it. And if you try to implement all ten opinions, you'll quickly end up with a total mess.

If most of your readers didn't understand your big plot reveal, it's probably confusing and worth revisiting. If only one person didn't get it, that person is probably an outlier.

You also need to filter comments by whether or not someone is your ideal reader and by how well they understand the tropes and expectations of your genre. Does the person giving you advice understand your genre? Is the advice specific to your work or situation? Are they just parroting rules they learned from "writing experts," or are they legitimately knowledgeable themselves?

In other words, if the person giving you advice on your romance novel's plot is a USA Today Best Selling Romance writer, listen to them! If they're an English lit major with three unfinished novels and no story sales, thank them and move the conversation on. If they primarily read and write literary fiction and complain that your epic fantasy has too many weird names and magic in it, the answer is probably not to simplify your complex world. If they primarily read and write thrillers and complain your memoir is too slow-moving, the answer is probably not to add more action scenes.

In both cases, the answer is to find a critique partner (or group, which we'll talk about in the next chapter) who understands your genre expectations and spend time building up trust with them.

## *Protecting Yourself*

I want to tell you that every person who crosses your path as you explore the writing community will be supportive, kind, and genuine. More often than not, that's true. But it's also important to develop a filter to protect yourself from bad actors.

There seem to be two camps about how to do this. (You probably fall into one or the other already.)

One camp employs a bouncer at the door, vetting every person with a critical eye before letting them come any closer. The other camp leaves the door wide open to anyone but has a robust right-to-refuse-service policy. In other words, the first camp views potential new friends as foe until proven friend, the second camp views them as friend until proven foe.

I lean toward the second camp, personally, and I know that stance is the result of a lot of privilege and good luck throughout my life. However you choose to vet potential new stars in your constellation, it's important to come up with your own criteria.

Many of these red flags are applicable to any friendship, but some are more specific to the writing community. If you notice these red flags, it doesn't mean you need to cut these people out of your life entirely, but it's probably smart to protect your energy and let them slip into a more distant orbit.

1. They take without giving. Are you always exhausted after you hang out with someone? Do you always feel like you're there to support them, to offer them favors, and to

listen to their problems—but they vanish the minute you need some help yourself?

2. You feel like you're being used for your position or contacts. This is the person who finds out you have an agent and immediately asks you for an introduction. Or who finds out you're an editor and immediately becomes your best friend.

3. They're always jealous of you. Like we just talked about, jealousy is a normal thing among writers. But when you tell a true friend about a win, they will genuinely celebrate with you. They'll see your hard work and effort and make you feel like you deserved it. If you're always finding yourself downplaying wins or avoiding sharing good news with someone, be very guarded with your energy around them.

4. They're dismissive of you (or others). Certain types of writers have a lot of ego about their work (read: their insecurity about their own work has built a protective ego wall), and

they've come to believe that there's only one way to do things. Only one "good" genre, only one "correct" stylistic choice, only one "right" way to publish your books. Don't give them the power to shape your own creative voice or career.

5. They're always complaining about others to you. If someone is always gossiping or complaining to you about other people, you can bet that they're also talking about you behind your back. Be extremely careful what you share with them.

6. They want you to be theirs exclusively. They're trying to isolate you from your other writer friends or groups by always talking bad about them, complaining about you spending time with them, or subtly sabotaging your relationships with others.

## Take Action

Who are the writer friends already in your constellation? Where do they fall in the Venn diagram of professional and personal relationships? Have any relationships shifted in ways that might require redrawing boundaries? Are there any places where you can see patterns or habits forming that might make things rocky further down the line?

If you like, you can even physically draw a Venn diagram to help you visualize this process.

If you've been throwing around ideas with a friend about starting a project together, schedule a time to nail down logistics and expectations, then jot down a list of to-dos, ideas, and concerns to bring to your logistics meeting.

Even if you're already working together, it's not too late to have a conversation about setting up protections around both your friendship and your business opportunity. (Including writing up a contract.)

And if you're noting jealousy or other uncomfortable feelings surfacing in your writer friendships, figure out how to handle that in a healthy way. Talk to your therapist, journal it out, and find ways to genuinely be happy for friends while staying encouraged on your own journey.

*Friending: Creating Meaningful, Lasting Adult Friendships* by Gina Handley Schmitt is an excellent resource for learning how to be a better friend in any context.

# CHAPTER 6: NAVIGATING GROUP RELATIONSHIPS

As I write this, I'm working on my first contemporary thriller novel. I've been playing in the sci-fi/fantasy sandbox for decades now, so I'm super familiar with the landscape of professional organizations, author groups, conferences, and social meetups. But I'm not really sure where the mystery kids hang out—so I asked a friend who's active in the Sisters in Crime organization for coffee so I could pick her brain.

Over the course of an hour, she exploded my world by telling me about the sheer number of different mystery writer associations, local and national conferences, online groups, and meetups I could join. It turns out there are three different professional organizations in Portland alone, which is absolutely wild. (And wonderful!)

My point is that there are an incredible number of possibilities when it comes to joining writing groups these days, no matter what you write or where you live (thank you, internet!). And each group has its very own culture—which means you have the opportunity to dip your toe in and see if the group dynamic is going to match your vibe or if you should keep shopping around.

My journey as a writer has been made all the more rich and wonderful because of the friends I've made along the way—and I truly believe that yours will be, too. But in a community as wide and varied as the writing world is, you're not going to be a great fit with everybody. And that's fine.

As I said earlier, you're at the center of your writing community constellation. You're in control of building your own ecosystem of writer friends and sub-groups. Don't let anyone make you feel like you have to leave behind your own values, voice, or creativity in order to join their group or friend circle. Whether you're in an online critique group, attending an in-person conference, or meeting up with a handful of people for a write-in, you get to decide what supports you and what's not your cup of tea.

When I say you're the center of your own constellation, I'm not giving you permission to act like the center of the world. Forming your own supportive constellation means being a stellar member of your friends' constellations, too. It's a give and take. You have to protect yourself against groups and people who are only there to take, of course. But in your vigilance, it's important not to become that person yourself.

As you navigate this world, how can you help every one of your writing friends and writing groups shine more brightly?

## *Finding the Right Fit*

I've been fortunate to link up with some incredible writing groups and organizations that have helped my career grow. But the reality is that not all groups are created equal. There are, unfortunately, a number of writing groups out there with toxic and/or exclusive cultures which deal critical damage to the writers who pass through them.

A toxic critique group can poison your love of writing. A predatory group leader can destroy your sense of self-worth. A narcissistic member can unravel a writing group, whether maliciously or out of habit.

I'm not saying this to scare you, but to help you protect yourself and your creative voice. You'll find dysfunctional communities and people in every hobby, profession, and fandom, and learning how to set strong boundaries and advocate for yourself is an important skill.

Newer writers who are just dipping their toes into finding community may join a group and think that the behavior they find there is standard. Au contraire. Each writing group has its own vibe and culture. If something's rubbing you the wrong way in one of them, you're free to walk away and find a group where the culture is a better fit for you.

Watch out for:

1. Cult of personality. Is the group organized around a revered leader whose instruction is considered the gold standard, to the exclusion of any other way of writing? Feel free to learn what you can from them, but don't get sucked into their vortex.
2. Tall poppy syndrome. Is there a tendency to try to keep everyone at the same level? As in, to downplay an individual's success and cut them down whenever they have a win? If you have to avoid talking about your successes in a group, they're not actually supportive of you.
3. Tolerant of predatory behavior. Unfortunately, some awful people use writing groups

as hunting grounds. (They can often come off as mentors, taking younger writers under their wings.) If you feel an off, predatory vibe from someone in the group and no one listens to your concerns, the whole group is probably a bad place to be.

4. Prescriptive advice. Do they tend to hand out blanket rules for writing, business, or your author career? Or are they sharing things they've personally found to work, and offering you suggestions instead of prescriptions?

5. Echo chamber. Some groups become an echo chamber, where they stop looking outside for new perspectives and just start parroting each other's ideas back to them. They can still be useful, but don't let yourself fall into the trap of closing down your mind to new perspectives.

6. Their way or the highway. I said it before, and I'll say it again. Don't join a cult! If any group insists that their way is the only way

of doing things or tries to isolate you from other writer friends or writing groups, be very, very careful.

7. Culture of complaint. Is it fashionable to complain about the state of the industry, constantly share bad news articles, and complain about other writers or writing groups? If every conversation in this group is a downer, that energy is going to worm its way into your overall writing life.
8. Toxic positivity. Of course, the flip side of a complaining culture is where everything needs to be happy and positive all the time, and there's no room for real talk. The writing journey is a struggle at times, and one of the best parts about having a writing community is being able to ask for—and receive—support when you need it.

Toxic online groups share these same red flags, though they're often amplified because people are more prone to say things they wouldn't say to someone's face.

The trouble is that when you're first starting out, the online groups that are most easily accessible (easiest to find, easiest to join without credentials) can also be the most toxic. I would recommend lurking for a bit if possible, and observe the culture before investing emotionally. The good news is that there are thousands—maybe hundreds of thousands—of individual online groups to join. When you learn to spot red flags early, you can brush the dust off your shoes on the doormat and run the other direction.

When you're evaluating an online group, specifically watch out for:

1. Dismissive and negative responses. How do people respond to each other? Do people answer questions supportively? Do they celebrate each others' wins? Does there seem to be genuine kindness and good rapport here? Or, are posters dismissive, rude, and discouraging to each other?
2. No moderator (or a bad one). A good online group shouldn't just be a free-for-all. There needs to be a code of conduct and strong

moderators who keep it feeling safe and welcoming to all.

## *Getting the Most from Critique Groups*

Critique groups are often the first type of formal writing groups people join, so I want to spend a bit of time talking about how to be in one. We've already talked about how to graciously give and receive feedback with a solo partner. That advice also applies to working in a group—with the additional layer that you're getting more critiques all at once.

There are pluses and minuses to this. On the one hand, you can easily see trends in the type of comments you get. If one reader says they were confused by a character's action, you might decide to ignore them. If everyone in your critique group made the same note, you should probably figure out how to make that part more clear.

On the other hand, though, you're also more likely to get criticism from people who aren't your ideal readers and who don't understand what you're trying to do. It's all good. Take what's useful, note any trends in the feedback, and discard what doesn't fit.

Note that most formal critique groups will have established guidelines around how they run each feedback session. One of the most popular is the Milford-style critique, where participants take turns speaking for a set amount of time, explaining what they feel worked about the story and pointing out problem areas (without offering solutions). Once all the critics have given feedback, the author then has a chance to respond and ask questions.

It's certainly a lesson in humility to listen to people pick apart your work in silence, and it's a skill to respond without getting defensive.

There are also a lot of limitations with this style of critique—especially in groups that don't have shared context, and the author is prohibited from speaking up to provide that context. For example, if the critic is reading the work of a marginalized writer through a white-centric lens or if the critic and the author are writing in genres with different reader expectations.

For more on avoiding this trap and running critique groups that are inclusive, I recommend reading *Craft in the Real World: Rethinking Fiction Writing and Workshopping* by Matthew Salesses.

### *Side Note*

**What If Someone Steals My Story?**

Newer writers often worry about a different type of protection for their creative work: What if they share a draft in a critique group and someone steals it?

I've heard this fear from so many people—but I've never actually heard of an instance where this happened.

There are billions of ideas out in the world and a billion more ways to execute on each idea. Even if you and I start with the exact same basis for a story, the versions we end up with will be uniquely ours. Don't worry about protecting your ideas—worry about developing your voice.

The idea of someone stealing your actual manuscript and passing it off as theirs is a bit more plausible. There are legitimate examples of fraudsters trying to pass off someone else's writing as their own (though normally this is work that's published elsewhere, rather than something that was filched from a friend or critique group).

Make sure you're in a critique group with writers you trust. Professional organizations all have policies in place to protect the intellectual property of their writers, and if you're in a casual group, you get to collectively set those expectations and guard against bad actors.

## *Being Professional at Social Groups and Write-Ins*

Writing is an interesting field, in that it's both a potential source of deep friendships, and—for many of us—a profession. We've already talked about how to navigate the challenges of personal and professional relationships within your writer friend constellation, but there are a few additional tips I'd like to share for being in social groups.

### Be Open to Meeting Everyone

Remember that the writers you meet are your collaborators and colleagues, not your competition. A supportive writing friend constellation lifts up all the points of light within it—so don't make a habit of dismissing anyone out of hand.

I've noticed at more traditional or literary conferences, people often come with the goal of meeting editors and agents to further their careers. I've been in conversations where people are constantly looking past me to see if someone "more important" has entered the room, or they interrupt me mid-sentence to excuse themselves when they spot that person. As a new writer, this was disheartening—I actually stopped attending conferences for a while.

And I've dipped my toe into more informal groups where everyone seems to be trying to cozy up to the more "successful" members of the group, or where members immediately dismiss you if you didn't attend the same writing workshop they did or get an MFA.

It's okay to attend a conference to meet editors and agents or join a group because you're hoping to network with a big-name author—but don't forget you also need to make genuine connections with other writers. Once you realize that other writers aren't competition to be kept at arm's length, you can relax and have fun—and that's when the magic happens.

### Don't Try to Sell Your Book

Just as other writers aren't your competition, they're also not your audience. Sure, they might pick up your book if it sounds interesting, but if your goal is to sell books, sign up for pitch sessions or book fairs. A writing conference or social group is not the place to sell your book to other writers. In fact, it can be a major turnoff if you're talking about your book the entire time.

This especially applies to professionals you might meet at networking events and conferences, like an agent or editor. Unless they explicitly ask you for details, don't assume that they're open for an impromptu pitch session. If you're interested in working with them and have built a rapport, it's okay to ask if it's appropriate to follow up and how best to do that. But never assume that they're open to new work.

### Keep it Together

We're all adults here. You probably know the effect a drink or two (or a gummy) has on you in a social event. Maybe one relaxes you and helps you be chattier, and two becomes bad news. Maybe you have zero tolerance and are better off soothing your social butterflies in a different way before jumping in to meet new people.

Know thyself, friend. And have a plan ahead of time to not put yourself in a spot where you regret something you said or did while under the influence.

### Protect Our Community

The writing community is an amazing place, filled with creative weirdos just like you and me. We're brought together by the same love—writing—and we share the same dreams, desires, and odd quirks. As you navigate these star-studded skies, don't only find ways to protect yourself.

Keep an eye on the others in our community.

If you're from a historically dominant group, educate yourself about the needs of historically minoritized groups, and speak up when you see potential issues. Learn how to be proactive about making spaces accessible and welcoming for everyone in our community, and educate yourself on how to helpfully and respectfully advocate for people who might be getting tired of advocating constantly for themselves. And if a friend trusts you enough to confide they've had a negative encounter with a person you have a high opinion of, trust them back.

As part of being an advocate for others, educate your friends. Don't keep quiet when you hear friends saying something harmful—share what you know with them or, if they push back, let them know you're not the right audience for their prejudice.

Watch out for your friends—current and future—at conferences and conventions. If you see someone sitting by themselves, invite them in. If you see someone dragging someone else down, let them know that behavior isn't okay with you. And don't leave your female friend alone in the elevator with the creep who's been following her all night.

Celebrate your writer friends. Share their work. Encourage them. Lift them up. Pour your light into your constellation—from close friends to distantly orbiting potential friends—and you'll be amazed how much energy, joy, and love will flow back your way.

None of us are perfect. But if we all commit to learning, growing, and having each other's backs, we can make this community pretty damn amazing.

Now go out and make yourself some friends!

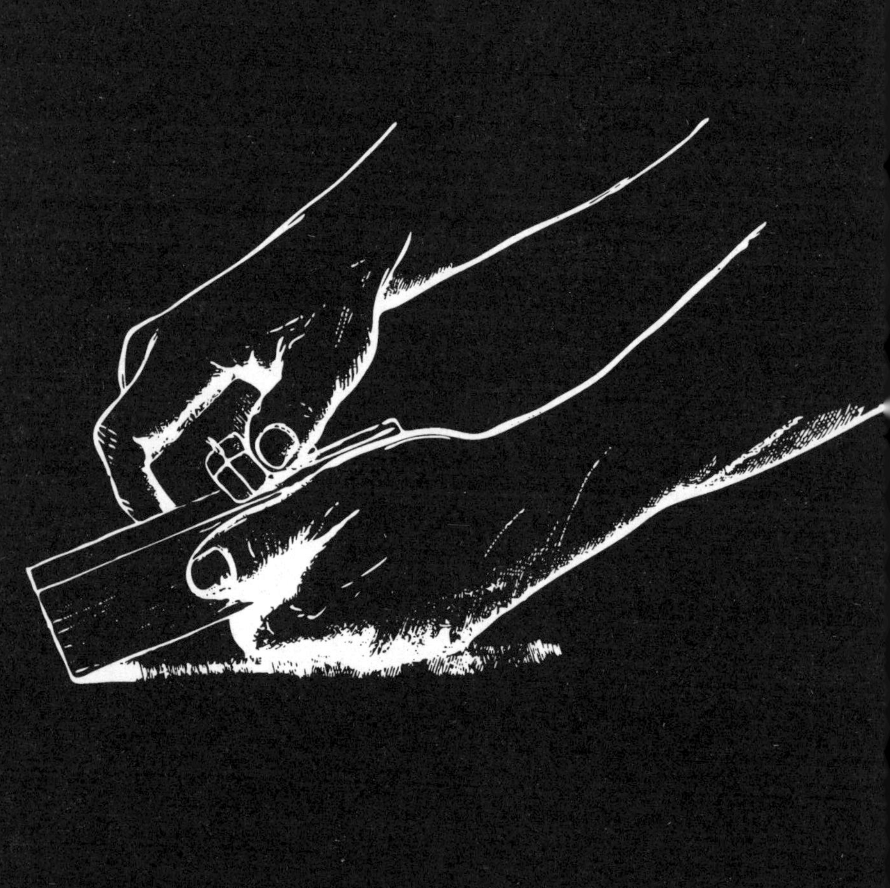

# RESOURCES

***Books mentioned:***

- *Unf#ck Your Brain: Getting over Anxiety, Depression, Anger, Freak-Outs, and Triggers with Science* by Dr. Faith G. Harper
- *Building a Second Brain: A Proven Method to Organize Your Digital Life and Unlock Your Creative Potential* by Tiago Forte
- *Friending: Creating Meaningful, Lasting Adult Friendships* by Gina Handley Schmitt
- *Craft in the Real World: Rethinking Fiction Writing and Workshopping* by Matthew Salesses

***Websites for finding conferences, courses, & community:***

- Poets & Writers: pw.org
- Writer's Digest: writersdigest.com
- Association of Writers & Writing Programs: awpwriter.org
- The Write Life: thewritelife.com
- Critique Circle: critiquecircle.com
- Alliance of Independent Authors: allianceindependentauthors.org

## *About the Author*

Jessie Kwak is an author, ghostwriter, and freelance marketing copywriter living in Portland, Oregon. As a writer, she sends readers on their own journeys to immersive worlds filled with fascinating characters, gunfights, and dinner parties. When she's not raving about her latest favorite sci-fi series to her friends, she can be found sewing, mountain biking, or out exploring new worlds both at home and abroad. She is the author of supernatural thriller *From Earth and Bone*, the Bulari Saga series of gangster sci-fi novels, and productivity guides *From Chaos to Creativity* and *From Big Idea to Book*. You can learn more about her at www.jessiekwak.com or follow her on Twitter (@jkwak).

# More books by

from www.Microcosm.Pub